BOOK ANALYSIS

Written by Mélanie Kuta
Translated by Rose Brichard

The Reader

BY BERNHARD SCHLINK

GW00499988

Bright
≡Summaries.com

BERNHARD SCHLINK

GERMAN WRITER

- **Born in Bielefed, Germany in 1944**
- **Notable works:**
  - *Self's Punishment* (2005), novel
  - *The Reader* (1995), novel
  - *The Weekend* (2010), novel

Born in Bielefeld, Germany in 1994, Bernhard Schlink is a judge and a law professor. He grew up in a protestant family. His father worked as a theology professor at a nearby university, but was called up during the war.

Schlink is the author of numerous crime novels, including a trilogy of works which all feature the same protagonist - a detective named Gerhard Selb. The Reader ("Der Vorleser" in German) was published in 1995, and made waves on the literary scene of the time. Schlink currently lives between Berlin and New York.

THE READER

THE WEIGHT OF HINDSIGHT

- **Genre:** novel
- **Reference edition:** Schlink, B. [no date] *The Reader*. [online]. Trans. Brown Janeway, C., New York: Vintage Books. [Accessed 14 July 2016]. Available from: <http://www.kkoworld.com/kitablar/bernhard_slink_qiraetci_kko-eng.pdf>.
- **First edition:** 1995
- **Themes:** World War II, Nazism, concentration camps, reading, illiteracy, shame

The Reader is a partly autobiographical novel first published in 1995 which was a true commercial success. It's a love story in three volumes which stretches over a 40-year time scale and is centred around a young German man and a former SS guard. The book raises the uncomfortable topic of concentration camps and the difficulties of remembering and discussing the two world wars faced by the generation of Germans who lived through them. The book is filled with feelings of shame and incomprehension.

Schlink's novel is short, written in a sobering and clear manner. Written in the first person, the narrator is also the protagonist. The book has been translated into 39 languages, and was the first German novel to shoot to the top of the *New York Times* bestsellers list.

SUMMARY

AN UNEXPECTED REUNION

Michael is a young law student. As part of one of his courses, a professor takes him and his class to a trial against former SS officers who had worked in concentration camps. To his great surprise, Michael sees a woman named Hanna, with whom he had had an affair a few years previously. She is one of the accused, along with four other women. He learns that Hanna had begun working for the SS as a guard in 1943 and worked in Auschwitz. The two major crimes she is accused of concern the selection process at the concentration camps during a night of bombing; the SS and the guards are accused of locking several hundred detainees in a church which caught fire amid the attack. Among all the deportees, only two women survived: a mother and daughter. They have written a book to immortalise their experience.

When the awful facts are said aloud, Michael feels nothing, numb to it all. Instead, it causes him to look back on his affair years before and this important part of his life.

INITIATION

One day when Michael is 15 and suffering from jaundice, he feels unwell and vomits on his way home from school. A woman named Hanna Schmitz, who is 20 years older than him, comes to his rescue and takes him back home. Once he feels better, Michael goes to her house to thank her. She welcomes him into her flat and gets changed in a room next door; Michael watches her out of the corner of his eye. Their eyes meet and, embarrassed, he runs away.

Eight days later, with Michael dreaming of Hanna every night, he decides to go back and see her once more. Madame Schmitz arrives home in a tramway worker's uniform. She sends Michael downstairs to get some coke (heating fuel), and when he emerges he is covered in sweat. She runs him a bath and he hesitantly undresses. She comes into the room naked, with a towel to wash him down. The two make love.

The following day, Michael goes back to school, but skips his afternoon classes to meet with his lover; this is his sexual awakening. One day, Hanna asks him to read a book. This is the start of a new ritual between the two - before they make love, Michael reads Hanna various different texts.

However, their relationship deteriorates little by little. Hanna is irritable and becomes distant; Michael fears he is losing her. During the Easter holidays, they go away together for four days on a bike ride. This escapade, helped particularly by the violent altercation which takes place during it, reawakens their passion.

THE DISAPPEARANCE

When Michael goes back to school, he changes class and takes a liking to a girl named Sophie. During the summer term, Michael begins to regret having spent so much time with Hanna when he could have been out having fun with his friends, who have been asking him about what he has been doing all this time.

A few days before the summer holidays, Michael notices that Hanna appears different and strange. One fine day, she disappears without a trace. Michael is devastated. He calls the tramway company where she works, and discovers that she quit her job just as they offered her a promotion to the level of driver.

Time passes and Michael manages to put Hanna out of his mind little by little. He finishes high school and goes to university to study law; fast-forward seven years and Hanna is still missing.

THE VERDICT

Back in the courtroom, Hanna tries to defend herself against the jury's accusations, some of which are false. Unlike most of the other defendants, Hanna admits that most of the events took place. The court also hears that Hanna had certain protégés in the camp who would read to her.

The presiding officer reads a report about the night of the bombings found in SS archives. The guards had deliberately locked the detainees in the church in the knowledge that they would die; the idea was to prevent any escape attempts. The other defendants deny all knowledge of such events and argue that Hanna alone wrote this false report. The presiding officer asks that Hanna's handwriting be checked against the report, but Hanna admits that she wrote it.

Michael can't stop thinking about Hanna's trial. He knows that she is illiterate, but also that he shouldn't reveal his former mistress's secret; he has to respect the choice she has made. He is nonetheless troubled by the whole affair, knowing that he has information that could change the outcome of the trial.

Michael decides to go to *Struthof*, the camp in question, to have a concrete image of the events discussed in the trial. He is truly moved by the scenes, and goes home in a state of shock, at once disgusted by Hanna and trying to understand her. Later on, the verdict is given and Hanna is sentenced to life, whereas the others have much lighter jail sentences.

Michael finishes university and begins his professional traineeship. He marries another trainee named Gertrude, and together they have a daughter named Julia. After five years of marriage, they divorce. When his years as a trainee are finally over, Michael chooses to specialise in legal history.

THE CASSETTE TAPES

One day, Michael decides to record himself reading aloud on cassette tapes. Several months later, he sends them to Hanna in prison. For ten years, he sends her recordings of novels, short stories, and even his own writing, though he never leaves her any personal messages. After four years, Hanna sends him a little note, then another one, about the books he has read to her. Michael sends her no reply, but realises that she must be learning to read by herself, matching up Michael's words with a print copy of the books from the prison library.

Eventually, he receives a letter from the head of the prison, informing him that Hanna is due for release. She asks him to help Hanna reintegrate into society after 18 years in jail. Michael goes to see Hanna a week before she is due to be released. She has aged dramatically, and the two discuss literature and the future.

The day of her release, Hanna commits suicide. The former SS had left Michael a letter, asking that he ensure that all her savings go to the one daughter who survived the fire in the church.

He agrees and goes to see the survivor in New York. She has difficulty understanding the relationship Michael bears to Hanna, who she sees as murderous, and refuses the money. She argues that taking money would be like forgiving Madame Schmitz, something she has no interest in. Instead, they decide to donate the money to a Jewish association helping to improve literacy.

Ten years later, Michael still thinks about Hanna, her death, and their affair. He decides to write their story down.

CHARACTER STUDY

MICHAEL BERG

In the first section of the novel, Michael is fifteen years old, living with his three brothers and sisters in a relatively well-off family. He is sickly, not very sure of himself and mediocre at school. However, this changes when he begins his secret affair with Hanna, as he gains some experience and self-assurance with regards to the people around him.

In the next section, Michael goes to university to study law. After Hanna's disappearance, Michael becomes more introverted and somewhat cuts himself off from the world. He is more cynical, and admits to feeling numb; he doesn't feel anything anymore, neither towards his old mistress nor towards the horrors of the wars. ("In every part of my life, too, I stood outside myself and watched; I saw myself functioning at the university, with my parents and brother and sister and my friends, but inwardly I felt no involvement..." p. 38).

In the third section, Michael continues to live in this "anesthetised" condition, running away from life's difficulties and burying himself in reading and writing. He decides to become a law historian instead of a judge. It is this same instinct to run away from problems that leads to his divorce from Gertrude.

Michael's entire life is shaped by his relationship with Hanna. These two characters personify the paradox which exists between two generations of Germans: the generation which lived through the war and Nazi rule - embodied by Hanna - and the generation which came after - Michael. Michael's generation can only try to come to terms with what their parents were part of.

HANNA SCHMITZ

Hanna was born in 1922 and grew up in Transylvania before moving to Berlin when she was 17 years old. She started working for Siemens before being recruited to work for the SS during the war.

In the first part of the book, she is 36 years old and works as a tramway conductor. She has an affair with Michael after the two meet by chance. She is a complex character and evolves throughout the novel. Her mood-swings leave Michael terrified of losing her. She has no family and always appears to be detached from reality. She is evasive and never gives direct answers to questions Michael asks her about her past.

She acts both as Michael's lover and his mother. On the surface, she is very sure of herself and assertive, dominating their relationship. However, she is hiding a great secret, her Achilles' heel: she is illiterate. She is ashamed of this and it prevents her from keeping her job after she is promoted for fear that her colleagues will find out. This is also why she asks Michael to read to her.

In the second section, Hanna is on trial. She is distant, perhaps even haughty, and speaks very little. She does not arouse feelings of sympathy among the audience-members. She shows herself to be naive, accepting all charges. She is very poorly-prepared for the trial due to her illiteracy.

In the third section, Hanna has aged dramatically and Michael struggles to see the woman he once loved in her. She chooses to hang herself over leaving prison.

Hanna is the personification of the generation which lived through the war and collaborated in the Nazi war effort, whether through action or inaction.

MICHAEL'S FATHER

Michael's father is a philosophy professor at the nearby university, specialising in Kant (German philosopher, 1724-1904) and Hegel (German philosopher, 1770-1831). He was stripped of his post during the war for giving lectures on Spinoza (Dutch philosopher, 1632-1677), and became the editorial director of a publishing house which printed trekking guides until the end of the war.

He makes appointments not only with his students but with his four children when any of them want to talk. He has a closed personality, and is incapable of expressing emotion. Michael tells the reader that his father doesn't care too much about his family members, seeing them rather as "pets" (p. 14).

MICHAEL'S MOTHER

Michael's mother only makes a very brief appearance in the

novel. One day, a psychoanalyst asks Michael to reflect on his mother's influence on his life, since she is almost absent from the story he has to tell.

SOPHIE

Sophie is one of Michael's school friends. She first appears in the novel when Michael's high school becomes mixed and she is part of his class. When he becomes friends with Sophie, Michael feels that he is betraying Hanna.

THE YOUNG JEWISH GIRL

This girl and her mother were the only people to escape from the horrors of the bombings at the concentration camp where Hanna worked. She writes a book about her experience and this leads to Hanna and her colleagues going on trial. She comes to give evidence during the case.

ANALYSIS

THE NEXT GENERATION AND THE WEIGHT OF THE PAST

The Reader raises many questions about the Second World war, the Nazi regime and the Holocaust. How should we talk about Nazi history in Germany? How can we understand what happened? How can we begin to forgive? The novel focuses especially on the difficulties faced by the generation whose parents participated in and lived through the war, as they try to come to terms with the recent past.

Feelings of shame are strongly present in the text. Young people feel ill-at-ease in the knowledge that their parents collaborated with the Nazis. The parents themselves are ashamed of what happened beneath their very eyes:

> "The generation that had been served by the guards and enforcers, or had done nothing to stop them, or had not banished them from its midst as it could have done after 1945, was in the dock, and we explored it, subjected it to trial by daylight, and condemned it to shame. Our parents had played a variety of roles in" (p. 34-35).
> "Whatever validity the concept of collective guilt may or may not have, morally and legally— for my generation of students it was a lived reality. It did not just apply to what had happened in the Third Reich...Pointing at the guilty parties did not free us from shame, but at least it overcame the suffering we went through on account of it. It converted the passive suffering of shame into energy, activity, aggression. And coming to grips with our parents' guilt took

a great deal of energy." (p. 60).

The love story between Michael and Hanna is a metaphor for this uncomfortable cohabitation between the two generations. He has difficulty feeling true anger towards the previous generation because of his love for Hanna, who had actively participated in the Holocaust.

> "I had to point at Hanna. But the finger I pointed at her turned back to me. I had loved her...I envied other students back then who had dissociated themselves from their parents and thus from the entire generation of perpetrators, voyeurs, and the wilfully blind, accommodators and accepters" (p. 60-61).

The key paradox of the novel lies therein; how can you love and hate your own parents and the same time? Is it possible to both judge and to understand?

> "I wanted simultaneously to understand Hanna's crime and to condemn it. But it was too terrible for that. When I tried to understand it, I had the feeling I was failing to condemn it as it must be condemned. When I condemned it as it must be condemned, there was no room for understanding." (p. 57)

The younger generation also struggle to deal with the huge mass of information on the Nazi period:

> "At the same time I ask myself, as I had already begun to ask myself back then: What should our second generation have done, what should it do with the knowledge of the horrors of the extermination of the Jews? We should not

believe we can comprehend the incomprehensible, we may not compare the incomparable, we may not inquire because to inquire is to make the horrors an object of discussion, even if the horrors themselves are not questioned, instead of accepting them as something in the face of which we can only fall silent in revulsion, shame, and guilt." (p.39)

Michael has trouble imagining Hanna's acts and understanding the true reality, since pictures and film footage of the Holocaust and the famous photos taken at the liberation of the camps have shaped his perception of events. Schlink presents the risk represented by true facts being transformed into still clichés, distorted by the collective imagination:

"I saw Hanna by the burning church, hard-faced, in a black uniform, with a riding whip... I knew that my fantasized images were poor clichés. They were unfair to the Hanna I had known and still knew... When I think today about those years, I realize how little direct observation there actually was, how few photographs that made life and murder in the camps real. We knew... the mountains of corpses found and photographed by the Allies at the liberation... Today there are so many books and films that the world of the camps is part of our collective imagination and completes our ordinary everyday one" (p. 53-54).

HANNA'S ILLITERACY

Hanna's illiteracy is one of the book's key topics, and Schlink uses it as a platform for exploring various important themes.

Hanna's inability to read or write can be read as a metaphor for modern failure or indeed efforts to comprehend the horrors of the Holocaust. Just as though they were illiterate, the after-war generation can see the facts, but they cannot understand them; they may be able to write about what happened, but they cannot truly come to terms with the reality of the Holocaust. When Michael reads the book written by the survivor of the bombing at the camp, he says:

> "Years later I reread it and discovered that it is the book that creates distance. It does not invite one to identify with it... It never gives the barracks leaders, the female guards, or the uniformed security force clear enough faces or shapes for the reader to be able to relate to them, to judge their acts for better or worse. It exudes the very numbness I have tried to describe before." (p. 44).

When Hanna is learning to read and write and finally leaves the realm of illiteracy, she understands her situation, and what really happened. It could be said that she too is awakening from an anaesthetic. When she understands the truth, she kills herself; she cannot live with the burden of this knowledge. She explains this to Michael:

> "I always had the feeling that no one understood me anyway, that no one knew who I was and what made me do this or that. And you know, when no one understands you, then no one can call you to account. Not even the court could call me to account. But the dead can. They understand. They don't even have to have been there, but if they were, they understand even better." (p. 69)

Hanna's illiteracy also allows Schlink to explore the theme of individual freedom. Amidst the collective guilt which permeated across the two generations in *The Reader*, freedom takes on a whole new level of importance.

During the trial, Michael realises that Hanna is illiterate; she could not have written the report. However, she would rather accept responsibility for the massacre than reveal her secret. Michael finds himself tempted to share this crucial information with the judge to show that while Hanna did play a terrible role in events that night, it was not as extreme as the one she was being charged with.

Troubled by this dilemma, he decides to speak with his father, who tells him:

> "Don't you remember how furious you would get as a little boy when Mama knew better what was good for you?... But with adults I see absolutely no justification for setting other people's views of what is good for them above their own ideas of what is good for themselves... We're not talking about happiness, we're talking about dignity and freedom." (p. 52)

Michael realises that he cannot force Hanna to talk, and must respect her wishes, her dignity and her freedom.

Lastly, Hanna's illiteracy is also connected to the theme of shame which flows throughout the novel. Hanna is ashamed of being illiterate and uneducated. To avoid being exposed, she constantly has to make changes in her life.

Many critics argue that through this, Schlink is trying to lessen Hanna's responsibility for her crimes; since she was illiterate, she had to join the SS. This begs the question -

could she possibly be forgiven? Does her illiteracy at some level explain her actions? There is a parallel to be drawn here with the entire wartime generation: were Germans forced to take part in the Nazi massacres? Does their ignorance of the true situation or their "illiteracy" somewhat diminish their responsibility? The author has no answers to these questions, and instead leaves the reader navigate this tricky moral playing field alone.

FURTHER REFLECTION

SOME QUESTIONS TO THINK ABOUT...

- In Schlink's novel, who is the reader? Is there more than one?
- At what exact moment did you realise Hanna is illiterate? Show how the author leaves different clues throughout the text which lead to this revelation.
- How is the fact that Hanna is illiterate important in the novel? What difference would it make if she knew how to read and write?
- The novel is divided into three sections: Hanna and Michael's love story, Hanna's trial, and her period of imprisonment. Does Schlink maintain the same writing style and tone throughout the three parts of the book?
- In your opinion, why does Hanna choose the youngest and weakest prisoners to read to her? Why did she decide to send them to Auschwitz?
- Why does Michael love Homer's *The Odyssey*? Discuss the different references made to this text in *The Reader* and explain their significance.
- "How could it be a comfort that the pain I went through because of my love for Hanna was, in a way, the fate of my generation, a German fate, and that it was only more difficult for me to evade, more difficult for me to manage than for others." (Michael, p. 61). Discuss.
- When Hanna is learning to read in prison, she mostly reads books about concentration camps. Did these books and the information they provide change Hanna's perception of her own actions during the war? How does

this lead to her suicide?

- Reread the chapter where Michael hitchhikes to the *Struthof* camp and the conversation he has with the driver in detail. Why does he discreetly kick Michael out of his vehicle? Why does Michael go to the camp in the first place? What does he hope to find there?
- Compare and contrast the novel with Stephen Daldry's film adaptation.
- Do you think that Germans being unaware of the extent of the situation under the Nazi regime, i.e. their "illiteracy" concerning the Holocaust, diminishes their responsibility? Justify your response.

We want to hear from you!
Leave a comment on your online library
and share your favourite books on social media!

FURTHER READING

REFERENCE EDITION:

- Schlink, B. (2010) *The Reader.* [online]. Trans. Janeway, C. B., New York: Vintage Books. [Accessed 14th July 2016]. Available from: <http://www.kkoworld.com/kitablar/ bernhard_slink_qiraetci_kko-eng.pdf>

REFERENCE STUDIES

- Niven, B. (2003) Bernhard Schlink's *Der Vorleser* and the Problem of Shame. *Modern Language Review*, Vol. 98(2), pp. 381-396.

FILM ADAPTATION

- *The Reader.* (2008) [Film]. Stephen Daldry. Dir. Germany & USA: Mirage Enterprises.

Printed in Great Britain
by Amazon